Axel Scheffler

Mother Goose's

Nursery Rhymes

and How She Came to Tell Them

with stories by
Alison Green

MACMILLAN CHILDREN'S BOOKS

For Clémentine – AS

First published 2006 by Macmillan Children's Books
a division of Macmillan Publishers Limited
20 New Wharf Road, London N1 9RR
Basingstoke and Oxford
Associated companies throughout the world
www.panmacmillan.com

ISBN: 978-0-333-96136-0

Text copyright © Macmillan Children's Books 2006
Illustrations copyright © Axel Scheffler 2006
The right of Axel Scheffler to be identified as the
Illustrator of this work has been asserted by him in accordance
with the Copyright Designs and Patents Act 1988.

5 7 9 8 6 4

A CIP catalogue record for this book is available from the British Library.

Printed in China

CONTENTS

One springtime Mother Goose laid three eggs. The first one to hatch was a boy. He had big flat feet and he was noisy. His mummy called him Boo.

One week later the second egg hatched. She was a girl. She had very flappy wings, and was almost as noisy as Boo. Her mummy called her Lucy.

They had to wait one more week for the last egg to hatch. It was another boy. He was shy and dreamy. His mummy called him Small. Boo, Lucy and Small. Mother Goose was very proud of them.

Mother Goose taught her goslings how to do all the things that geese do: how to nibble at the soft wet grass; how to swim up and down the great wide river; how to duck their heads under the water looking for waterweed; how to sleep on one leg on the riverbank. That was hard.

Most of all, she taught them how to waddle along behind her in a row: *waddle*-waddle, *waddle*-waddle, *waddle*-waddle . . .

"Keep up, Small," called Mother Goose, when Small stopped to stare at butterflies.

And, "Boo, don't splash!" when Boo jumped in a puddle.

And, "Waddle nicely, Lucy!" when Lucy kept flapping at wasps.

And, "Keep together, everyone," when all the goslings waddled off in different directions.

It wasn't easy looking after goslings.

So Mother Goose started to tell them rhymes: happy rhymes, sad rhymes, silly rhymes, rhymes to wave their wings about to, rhymes to lull them to sleep.

After that, whenever Small stopped to stare at a butterfly,

or Lucy wandered off to look at a beetle, or Boo saw a puddle that was just waiting to be jumped in, Mother Goose told them a rhyme, and they all waddled on just as they should.

They were such good rhymes that soon other mother geese started telling them to their goslings, too. So did the coots and the mallards and the moorhens, even the voles and the water rats, all along the river. At last, a wise old heron wrote the rhymes down in this book, so that children everywhere could enjoy them.

The goslings were having a sleepy morning.

"Time to get up!" called Mother Goose. "Breakfast time!"

"I'm tired, Mummy," said Lucy.

"So am I," said Small.

"So am I," said Boo.

"Oh dear," said Mother Goose. "We must have waddled too far yesterday. I've got an idea. Let's wait a bit and watch the trains go by before we have breakfast."

The goslings loved watching the trains. After they'd watched five trains go by Mother Goose said, "Shall we be a train, now, chugging all the way down to the river? I'll be the engine, and you be the carriages following behind me."

"Can I say, 'Off we go'?" asked Lucy.

"Yes, you can," said Mother Goose. "And Boo and Small can make all the train noises."

So Lucy shouted, "One, two, three – off we go!" and Boo and Small shouted, "Chug-chug!" and "Toot-toot!" all the way to the river.

DOWN BY THE STATION

Down by the station
Early in the morning,
See the little puffer trains
All in a row.
   See the engine driver
   Turn the little handle.
   Chug-chug,
   Toot-toot,
Off we go.

One Misty, Moisty Morning

One misty, moisty morning,
When cloudy was the weather,
There I met an old man
Clothed all in leather;
Clothed all in leather,
With cap under his chin.
How do you do, and how do you do,
And how do you do again?

Chook, Chook, Chook

Chook, chook, chook, chook, chook,

Good morning, Mrs Hen.

How many chickens have you got?

Madam, I've got ten.

Four of them are yellow,

And four of them are brown,

And two of them are speckled red,

The nicest in the town.

ELSIE MARLEY

Elsie Marley is grown so fine,

She won't get up to feed the swine,

But lies in bed till eight or nine.

Lazy Elsie Marley.

"We get up early, don't we, Mummy?" said Lucy.

"Yes, we do," said Mother Goose. "You woke me up at five o'clock this morning. That's very early."

"But we don't have to feed any swine," said Small.

"No, you just bounce up and down on top of me till I wake up."

"Don't you like that, Mummy?" asked Boo.

"Sometimes I like it," said Mother Goose. "But sometimes I think it would be rather nice to stay in bed till eight or nine."

"No, it wouldn't!" shouted the goslings.

"Yes, it would!" said Mother Goose.

"Lazy Mummy!" said Lucy. "We'd better wake you up at four o'clock tomorrow!"

"Don't you dare!" laughed Mother Goose.

Pat-a-cake

Clap along with the rhyme!

Pat-a-cake, pat-a-cake, baker's man,

Bake me a cake as fast as you can;

Pat it and prick it, and mark it with B,

Put it in the oven for baby and me.

PEASE PORRIDGE

This is another good rhyme to clap along to.

Pease porridge hot,
Pease porridge cold,
Pease porridge in the pot
Nine days old.

Some like it hot,
Some like it cold,
Some like it in the pot
Nine days old.

As I Went to Bonner

As I went to Bonner,
I met a pig
Without a wig,
Upon my word and honour.

"I've never seen a pig in a wig," said Mother Goose. "Have you?"

"Yes, I have!" said Boo.

"No, you haven't," said Lucy.

"I have," said Boo. "Down by the willow tree last week. It barked at us."

"That wasn't a pig in a wig," laughed Lucy. "That was a shaggy dog."

"Pigs don't bark," said Small. "They go oink."

"They bark when they're wearing wigs," said Boo, and he hid behind some ferns, sulking.

"Don't worry," said Mother Goose. "He'll come out when he's hungry."

Boo ran out from behind his ferns. "Did someone say hungry?" he panted.

"Yes," laughed Mother Goose. "I think it's dinner time! Come on, everyone," and they all sploshed into the river.

JERRY HALL

Jerry Hall,

He is so small,

A rat could eat him,

Hat and all.

LITTLE POLL PARROT

Little Poll Parrot
Sat in his garret
Eating toast and tea;
A little brown mouse,
Jumped into the house,
And stole it all away.

Row, Row, Row Your Boat

Row, row, row your boat

Gently down the stream.

Merrily, merrily, merrily, merrily,

Life is but a dream.

The goslings were having a swimming lesson.

"I like that rhyme," sighed Small. "I wish we had a boat to row. It would be much easier than swimming."

"I know some different words to that rhyme," said Boo. "They go like this," and he sang:

"Row, row, row your boat,
Gently down the stream.
If you see a crocodile,
Don't forget to scream!"

"Crocodile!" screamed Small. He scrambled out of the water as fast as he could, and wouldn't come back in.

"Come on, Small," called Mother Goose. "There aren't any crocodiles in this river."

But Small wouldn't come back until Mother Goose waddled out and gave him a cuddle.

"Let's just sing my words in future, shall we?" she said.

HICKETY, PICKETY, MY BLACK HEN

Hickety, pickety, my black hen,
She lays eggs for gentlemen;
Gentlemen come every day
To see what my black hen doth lay.
Sometimes nine and sometimes ten,
Hickety, pickety, my black hen.

COCK-A-DOODLE-DOO!

Cock-a-doodle-doo!
My dame has lost her shoe,
My master's lost his fiddling stick,
And knows not what to do.

RIDE A COCK-HORSE

Ride a cock-horse to Banbury Cross,

To see a fine lady upon a white horse;

Rings on her fingers and bells on her toes,

And she shall have music wherever she goes.

I Had a Little Horse

I had a little horse,

His name was Dappled Grey.

His head was made of gingerbread,

His tail was made of hay.

He could amble, he could trot,

He could carry the mustard pot,

He could amble, he could trot,

Through the old Town of Windsor.

Boo was jumping in puddles again.

"One, two, three . . . SPLASH! One, two, three . . . SPLASH!"

"Mummy!" wailed Lucy. "Boo keeps splashing me."

"Boo," said Mother Goose. "How many times have I told you not to splash?"

"Lots of times," said Boo.

"So you won't do it again, will you?" said Mother Goose.

"Just one more time," said Boo. "Just that puddle over there . . ."

Before Mother Goose could stop him, Boo went, "One, two, three . . . KER–SPLOSH!" right into the deepest puddle you ever saw.

Boo came up coughing and crying.

"Oh dear," said Mother Goose. "I'd better tell you a rhyme to cheer you up. It's called *Doctor Foster*," she said, "and it's about a very big puddle indeed."

DOCTOR FOSTER

Doctor Foster went to Gloucester

In a shower of rain;

He stepped in a puddle,

Right up to his middle,

And never went there again.

As I Was Going to St Ives

As I was going to St Ives,

I met a man with seven wives,

Each wife had seven sacks,

Each sack had seven cats,

Each cat had seven kits:

Kits, cats, sacks, and wives,

How many were there going to St Ives?

Answer: one! All the others were coming from St Ives.

A Man in the Wilderness

A man in the wilderness asked me,
How many strawberries grow in the sea?
I answered him, as I thought good,
As many as red herrings grow in the wood.

GEORGIE PORGIE

Georgie Porgie, pudding and pie,
Kissed the girls and made them cry;
When the boys came out to play,
Georgie Porgie ran away.

 "I wouldn't kiss girls," said Boo. "Kissing's yucky."

"You kiss Mummy," said Lucy. "You kiss her goodnight every night."

"That's different," said Boo. "I wouldn't kiss *you*."

"Well I'll just have to kiss *you,* then," said Lucy.

"Oh, no, you won't!" shouted Boo, and he ran off and hid in an old bucket.

"I'm still going to kiss you," said Lucy, and she started kissing the bucket.

"Mummy!" cried Boo. "Lucy's kissing the bucket!"

"Don't kiss the bucket, Lucy," said Mother Goose. "You don't know where it's been."

"But Boo won't come out," said Lucy.

"He doesn't want to be kissed, darling," said Mother Goose. "Boo, come out, now, and we'll all sing a playing rhyme together."

So they sang *Boys and Girls, Come Out to Play* . . .

Boys and Girls, Come Out to Play

Boys and girls, come out to play,

The moon doth shine as bright as day.

Leave your supper and leave your sleep,

And join your playfellows in the street.

Come with a whoop and come with a call,

Come with a good will or not at all.

Up the ladder and down the wall,

A half-penny loaf will serve us all;

You find milk, and I'll find flour,

And we'll have a pudding in half an hour.

Little Jack Horner

Little Jack Horner
Sat in the corner,
Eating a Christmas pie;
He put in his thumb,
And pulled out a plum,
And said, What a good boy am I!

Lavender's Blue

Lavender's blue, diddle, diddle,
    Lavender's green;
When I am king, diddle, diddle,
    You shall be queen.

Call up your men, diddle, diddle,
    Set them to work,
Some to the plough, diddle, diddle,
    Some to the cart.

Some to make hay, diddle, diddle,
    Some to thresh corn,
Whilst you and I, diddle, diddle,
    Keep ourselves warm.

"When I'm king," said Boo, "I'll set you all to work. I'll sit on the riverbank, and you'll have to fetch weed for me to eat, and bring it on a silver platter."

"You'll get very fat," said Mother Goose, "if you don't run around and swim."

"And you won't be able to jump in puddles," said Lucy.

"Kings aren't allowed to jump in puddles," said Small.

"Are kings allowed to play games?" asked Boo.

"Only chess," said Lucy. "And crosswords."

"And they have to be in a bad mood all day long, and make up rules for everyone," said Small.

"When are you going to be king?" asked Lucy.

"Oh, not for ages," said Boo. "I'll let you know."

LITTLE BOY BLUE

Little Boy Blue,
    Come blow your horn,
The sheep's in the meadow,
    The cow's in the corn;
But where is the boy
    Who looks after the sheep?
He's under a haycock,
    Fast asleep.
Will you wake him?
    No, not I,
For if I do,
    He's sure to cry.

WILLY BOY, WILLY BOY

Willy boy, Willy boy, where are you going?
    I will go with you, if that I may.
I'm going to the meadow to see them a-mowing,
    I am going to help them to make the hay.

Baa, Baa, Black Sheep

Baa, baa, black sheep,
    Have you any wool?
Yes, sir, yes, sir,
    Three bags full;
One for the master,
    And one for the dame,
And one for the little boy
    Who lives down the lane.

IF I HAD A DONKEY

If I had a donkey that wouldn't go,

Would I beat him? Oh no, no.

I'd put him in the barn and give him some corn,

The best little donkey that ever was born.

Small was puzzled.

"Mummy," he said. "Why am I a goose?"

"Because I'm a goose," said Mother Goose, "and you're my baby."

"Ah," said Small. Then he said, "Mummy, why have I got big feet?"

"Because I've got big feet," said Mother Goose, "and you're just like me."

"Ah," said Small. Then he said, "Mummy, why have you got a long neck but I've only got a short neck?"

"You'll have a long neck when you're a big goose," said Mother Goose.

"Ah," said Small. Then he said, "Mummy, when I'm a big goose, will I know all about everything, just like you do?"

"Of course," said Mother Goose. "If you remember everything I tell you."

"How will I do that?" said Small.

"Well," said Mother Goose, "you could try and be like the wise old owl in this rhyme . . ."

A WISE OLD OWL

A wise old owl sat in an oak,

The more he heard the less he spoke;

The less he spoke the more he heard.

Why aren't we all like that wise old bird?

LITTLE JACK SPRAT

Little Jack Sprat
Once had a pig;
It was not very little,
Not yet very big,
It was not very lean,
It was not very fat –
It's a good pig to grunt,
Said little Jack Sprat.

THIS LITTLE PIG

Starting with the big toe, pretend each of your gosling's toes is a little pig. On the last line, tickle her under the foot.

This little pig went to market,

This little pig stayed at home,

This little pig had roast beef,

This little pig had none,

And this little pig cried, Wee-wee-wee-wee-wee,

    All the way home.

How Many Miles to Babylon?

How many miles to Babylon?

Three score miles and ten.

Can I get there by candlelight?

Yes, and back again.

If your heels are nimble and light,

You may get there by candlelight.

"How far is a mile?" asked Boo.

"A mile is a long way to waddle," said Mother Goose.

"Is it as far as that gate-post?" asked Small.

"It's much further than that," said Mother Goose.

"Gosh," said Small.

"So, how far is three score miles and ten?" asked Lucy.

"That's even further," said Mother Goose.

"Could we get there by candlelight?" asked Boo.

"Geese don't have candles," said Mother Goose. "But we could get there by flying. Geese can fly ever so far."

"Flying's too hard," said Small. "I'm never going to fly."

"You just have to practise," said Mother Goose. "Then you can fly anywhere you want."

"Even to Babylon?" asked Lucy.

"Even to Babylon," said Mother Goose.

So they all practised flapping their wings.

There Was a Crooked Man

There was a crooked man,
　　and he walked a crooked mile,
He found a crooked sixpence
　　against a crooked stile;
He bought a crooked cat,
　　which caught a crooked mouse,
And they all lived together
　　in a little crooked house.

RUB-A-DUB-DUB

Rub-a-dub-dub,
Three men in a tub,
And who do you think they be?
The butcher, the baker,
The candlestick-maker,
Turn 'em out, knaves all three.

HUMPTY DUMPTY

Humpty Dumpty sat on a wall,

Humpty Dumpty had a great fall.

All the king's horses,

And all the king's men,

Couldn't put Humpty together again.

"W as Humpty Dumpty an egg, Mummy?" asked Boo.

"Yes, he was," said Mother Goose. "But he wasn't a very sensible egg."

"Why?" asked Boo.

"Because he sat on a wall," said Mother Goose. "That's not a safe place for an egg."

"What is a safe place for an egg?" asked Boo.

"In a nest," said Mother Goose. "When you were eggs, I kept you all safe in a nest until you hatched."

"If Humpty Dumpty had hatched, would he have been a goose?" asked Boo.

"I don't think so," said Mother Goose. "He wasn't that sort of egg."

"What sort of egg was he?" asked Boo.

"The sort that wears clothes and sits on a wall," said Mother Goose.

"That's a silly sort of egg," said Boo.

"Yes," said Mother Goose. "It is."

Jack and Jill

Jack and Jill went up the hill
    To fetch a pail of water;
Jack fell down and broke his crown,
    And Jill came tumbling after.

There Was an Old Woman

There was an old woman
Lived under a hill,
And if she's not gone
She lives there still.

Ring-a-ring o' Roses

All hold hands and skip round in a ring.
On the last line, all sit down on the ground.

Ring-a-ring o' roses,

A pocket full of posies.

A-tishoo! A-tishoo!

We all fall down.

The goslings had been playing ring o' roses all morning. They were all rather dizzy.

"Ring-a-ring-a-ring-a-ring-a-ring," sang Small, spinning round in circles. Then he fell down on his bottom with a bump.

Lucy and Boo did the same, and soon they were all lying in a heap, giggling.

"Oh dear," said Mother Goose. "This doesn't look like the best time to start your flying lessons."

"We can do flying tomorrow – hic!" said Lucy. She'd laughed so much she'd got hiccups.

"Sing us another rhyme, Mummy," said Small.

"Very well," sighed Mother Goose. "I'll sing you one where you have to wave your wings about. At least that will make them strong for flying. It's called *Incey Wincey Spider* . . ."

Incey Wincey Spider

Join in the actions!

Incey wincey spider

Climbing up the spout;

*Use all your fingers to show
how the spider climbs up.*

Down came the rain

And washed the spider out:

*Wriggle your fingers down
to show the rain.*

Out came the sun

And dried up all the rain;

*Sweep your hands up and
bring them out and down.*

Incey wincey spider

Climbing up again.

*Do the same as for the
first verse.*

Ladybird, Ladybird

Ladybird, ladybird,
Fly away home,
Your house is on fire
And your children all gone;
All except one
And that's little Ann
And she has crept under
The warming pan.

LITTLE BO-PEEP

Little Bo-peep has lost her sheep,
And can't tell where to find them;
Leave them alone, and they'll come home,
And bring their tails behind them.

Little Bo-peep fell fast asleep,
And dreamt she heard them bleating;
But when she awoke, she found it a joke,
For they were still all fleeting.

Then up she took her little crook,
Determined for to find them;
She found them indeed, but it made her heart bleed,
For they'd left their tails behind them.

It happened one day, as Bo-peep did stray

Into a meadow hard by,

There she espied their tails side by side,

All hung on a tree to dry.

She heaved a sigh, and wiped her eye,

And over the hillocks went rambling,

And tried what she could, as a shepherdess should,

To tack again each to its lambkin.

Mother Goose was teaching the goslings how to count.

"If I have three eggs, and two of them hatch, how many eggs have I got left? Small?"

But Small was looking at the lambs in the field. "Look, Mummy!" he said. "That lamb's got a wiggly tail."

"So has that one," said Lucy.

"That makes two lambs with wiggly tails," said Boo.

"That's right, Boo," said Mother Goose. "I'm glad one of you can count."

"I can count!" said Small.

"Go on, then," said Mother Goose.

"One lamb, two lambs," said Small.

"Can you count the trees?" asked Mother Goose.

"No," said Small. "Just the lambs."

"Can we have a rhyme about a lamb, please, Mummy?" asked Lucy.

"All right, then," sighed Mother Goose. "Then we really must do some more counting."

MARY HAD A LITTLE LAMB

Mary had a little lamb,

Its fleece was white as snow;

And everywhere that Mary went

The lamb was sure to go.

It followed her to school one day,

That was against the rule;

It made the children laugh and play

To see a lamb at school.

ONE, TWO, THREE, FOUR

One, two, three, four,

Mary at the cottage door,

Five, six, seven, eight,

Eating cherries off a plate.

One, Two, Three, Four, Five

One, two, three, four, five,

Once I caught a fish alive,

Six, seven, eight, nine, ten,

Then I let it go again.

Why did you let it go?

Because it bit my finger so.

Which finger did it bite?

This little finger on the right.

If All the Seas Were One Sea

If all the seas were one sea,

What a *great* sea that would be!

If all the trees were one tree,

What a *great* tree that would be!

And if all the axes were one axe,

What a *great* axe that would be!

And if all the men were one man,

What a *great* man that would be!

And if the *great* man took the *great* axe,

And cut down the *great* tree,

And let it fall into the *great* sea,

What a splish-splash that would be!

"If all the geese were one goose," said Boo, "that would be a really ginormous huge goose, wouldn't it?"

"Yes," said Mother Goose.

"When he waddled the ground would shake," said Lucy.

"That's right," said Mother Goose.

"And when he said, 'Honk!' it would sound like a trumpet," said Boo.

"It would," said Mother Goose.

"And when he flapped his wings, all the trees would fall down," said Lucy.

"That would be scary," said Mother Goose.

"I think geese are best being normal size," said Small.

"I think so, too," said Mother Goose.

THREE WISE MEN OF GOTHAM

Three wise men of Gotham,
They went to sea in a bowl,
And if the bowl had been stronger
My song had been longer.

There Was an Old Woman Called Nothing-at-all

There was an old woman called Nothing-at-all,

Who lived in a dwelling exceedingly small;

A man stretched his mouth to its utmost extent,

And down at one gulp house and old woman went.

SING, SING, WHAT SHALL I SING?

Sing, sing, what shall I sing?

The cat's run away with the pudding string!

Do, do, what shall I do?

The cat has bitten it quite in two!

Who's That Ringing?

Who's that ringing at my door bell?
  A little pussy cat that isn't very well.
Rub its little nose with a little mutton fat,
  For that's the best cure for a little pussy cat.

I t was a bright night, with the moon shining fat and round in the sky.

"Have you noticed how the moon gets bigger and smaller?" asked Mother Goose. The goslings had. "Sometimes it's big and fat like this, then it gets smaller and smaller, till all you can see is a thin little crescent moon."

"Then it gets big again," said Small.

"That's right," said Mother Goose.

"Mummy," said Lucy, "Where does the Man in the Moon go when the moon gets too small for him?"

"He comes down to Earth," said Mother Goose, "and goes on holiday to Norwich."

"Why does he go to Norwich?" asked Boo.

"He likes it there," said Mother Goose. "Except for one time, when he came down too soon. There's a rhyme about it . . ."

THE MAN IN THE MOON

The man in the moon

Came down too soon,

And asked his way to Norwich;

He went by the south,

And burnt his mouth

With supping cold plum porridge.

Hey Diddle Diddle

Hey diddle diddle,

The cat and the fiddle,

The cow jumped over the moon;

The little dog laughed

To see such sport,

And the dish ran away with the spoon.

HUSH-A-BYE, BABY

Hush-a-bye, baby, on the tree top,

When the wind blows the cradle will rock;

When the bough breaks the cradle will fall,

Down will come baby, cradle and all.

GRAY GOOSE AND GANDER

Gray goose and gander
Waft your wings together,
And carry the good king's daughter
Over the one-strand river.

"That's what I'm going to do when I grow up," said Boo. "I'm going to carry princesses over rivers."

"I thought you were going to be king," said Mother Goose.

"That's later on," said Boo.

"I'll help you carry them," said Lucy. "You can't carry a whole princess on your own."

"But I'd fly faster than you," said Boo, "so the princess would fall down and go splosh into the river."

"Then I'd have to rescue her," said Small.

"We'd all have to rescue her," said Boo. "Then we'd take her to the king."

"And he'd be really grateful, wouldn't he, Mummy?" said Lucy. "And he'd pay us lots of money."

"He'd probably be more grateful if you hadn't dropped her in the river," said Mother Goose.

"We'd flap our wings at her to dry her out," said Boo.

"Well that's all right, then," said Mother Goose.

Sing a Song of Sixpence

Sing a song of sixpence,
   A pocket full of rye;
Four and twenty blackbirds,
   Baked in a pie.

When the pie was opened,
   The birds began to sing;
Was not that a dainty dish,
   To set before the king?

The king was in his counting-house,
　　Counting out his money;
The queen was in the parlour,
　　Eating bread and honey.

The maid was in the garden,
　　Hanging out the clothes,
Along came a blackbird,
　　And snapped off her nose.

LITTLE MISS MUFFET

Little Miss Muffet
Sat on a tuffet,
Eating her curds and whey;
There came a big spider,
Who sat down beside her
And frightened Miss Muffet away.

"You be Miss Muffet, Small," said Boo, "and I'll be the spider."

"All right," said Small.

"You have to sit on a tuffet," said Boo. "That means grass."

"All right," said Small, and he sat down on the grass.

"Now you have to eat curds and whey," said Boo.

"I haven't got any," said Small.

"You have to pretend."

Small pretended. Boo sat down next to him.

"You're supposed to scream and run away," said Boo.

"Why?"

"Because I'm a big scary spider," said Boo.

"I thought you were a goose," said Small. "I thought we all were."

"We *are* geese!" said Boo. "I'm just pretending to be a spider. Mummy! Small doesn't know how to play pretending."

"Then let's play a game we all know," said Mother Goose. "How about *Two Little Dicky Birds* . . ."

Two Little Dicky Birds

Join in the actions! Use your two
index fingers to be Peter and Paul.

Two little dicky birds,

Sitting on a wall;

One named Peter,

The other named Paul.

Waggle each finger in turn.

Fly away, Peter!

Put "Peter" behind your back.

Fly away, Paul!

Put "Paul" behind your back.

Come back, Peter!

Come back, Paul!

Bring each finger back in front of you.

I Had a Little Hen

I had a little hen,
The prettiest ever seen,
She washed me the dishes
And kept the house clean.
She went to the mill
To fetch me some flour,
She brought it home
In less than an hour.
She baked me my bread,
She brewed me my ale,
She sat by the fire
And told many a fine tale.

I Had a Little Nut Tree

I had a little nut tree,
    Nothing would it bear
But a silver nutmeg
    And a golden pear;
The King of Spain's daughter
    Came to visit me,
And all for the sake
    Of my little nut tree.

Small was standing by a hazelnut tree.

"If I stand here, Mummy, will the King of Spain's daughter come and visit me?"

"Of course not, silly," said Lucy. "She's not going to come all that way for any old nut tree. You have to have a silver nutmeg and a golden pear."

Small looked sad.

"I'll come and visit you," said Mother Goose.

"Thank you," said Small.

"And, look," said Mother Goose. "This little robin's come to visit you, too."

"I knew it was worth standing by this nut tree!" said Small.

HECTOR PROTECTOR

Hector Protector was dressed all in green;

Hector Protector was sent to the Queen.

The Queen did not like him,

No more did the King;

So Hector Protector was sent back again.

OLD KING COLE

Old King Cole was a merry old soul,

And a merry old soul was he;

He called for his pipe,

And he called for his bowl,

And he called for his fiddlers three.

Each fiddler he had a fiddle,

And the fiddles went tweedle-dee;

Oh, there's none so rare as can compare

With King Cole and his fiddlers three.

Here We Go Round the Mulberry Bush

Here we go round the mulberry bush,
The mulberry bush, the mulberry bush,
Here we go round the mulberry bush,
On a cold and frosty morning.

This is the way we wash our hands,
Wash our hands, wash our hands,
This is the way we wash our hands,
On a cold and frosty morning.

This is the way we wash our clothes,
Wash our clothes, wash our clothes,
This is the way we wash our clothes,
On a cold and frosty morning.

"This is the way we fish for weed, fish for weed, fish for weed," sang Lucy, dunking her head in the water. She came up again a moment later, coughing and spluttering.

"Eat first, dear," said Mother Goose, "and then sing. You can't do both at once."

"I can if I practise," said Lucy.

"I don't think so, dear," said Mother Goose, but it was too late. Lucy had already ducked under the water, and bubbles were rising up where she was singing.

A few seconds later she was up again, coughing so hard she went bright red in the beak.

"A bit of weed went down the wrong way," she gasped.

"Oh, I see," said Mother Goose. "I thought it was the singing that made you cough."

"Oh, no," said Lucy, and she sang, "This is the way we cough up weed, cough up weed, cough up weed –"

"Those aren't the nicest words to sing, dear," said Mother Goose. "How about I sing you an eating song while you have your lunch? It's called *Polly Put the Kettle On* . . ."

Polly Put the Kettle On

Polly put the kettle on,
Polly put the kettle on,
Polly put the kettle on,
 We'll all have tea.

Sukey take it off again,
Sukey take it off again,
Sukey take it off again,
 They've all gone away.

Blow the fire and make the toast,
Put the muffins on to roast,
Who is going to eat the most?
 We'll all have tea.

I'm a Little Teapot

Join in with the actions!

I'm a little teapot, short and stout;

Here's my handle, here's my spout.

> *Put one hand on your hip, and hold the other out like the spout of a teapot.*

When I see the teacups, hear me shout,

"Tip me up and pour me out."

> *Lean over towards your "spout" arm, as if you're pouring out tea.*

THE NORTH WIND DOTH BLOW

The north wind doth blow,

And we shall have snow,

And what will poor robin do then?

    Poor thing.

He'll sit in a barn,

And keep himself warm,

And hide his head under his wing.

    Poor thing.

Three Little Kittens

Three little kittens they lost their mittens,
    And they began to cry,
Oh, mother dear, we sadly fear
    That we have lost our mittens.
What! lost your mittens, you naughty kittens!
    Then you shall have no pie.
    Mee-ow, mee-ow, mee-ow.
    No, you shall have no pie.

The three little kittens they found their mittens,
    And they began to cry,
Oh, mother dear, see here, see here,
    For we have found our mittens.
Put on your mittens, you silly kittens,
    And you shall have some pie.
    Purr-r, purr-r, purr-r,
    Oh, let us have some pie.

The goslings were not waddling nicely. Boo kept tickling Lucy, Lucy kept nipping Small's tail, Small kept tripping over his feet, and they all kept falling over in heaps of giggles.

"I don't know what's wrong with you today," said Mother Goose. "You're all just being silly."

"I'm not being silly," said Lucy, lying on her back and waving her feet in the air.

"Neither are we!" said Small and Boo, copying Lucy.

"Right," said Mother Goose. "This should make you behave. We're going to sing a marching song, and I want you all to act like soldiers."

"Oh, yes!" cried the goslings. They jumped to their feet and marched along, as Mother Goose sang *The Grand Old Duke of York* . . .

THE GRAND OLD DUKE OF YORK

Oh, the grand old Duke of York,
    He had ten thousand men;
He marched them up to the top of the hill,
    And he marched them down again.
And when they were up, they were up,
    And when they were down, they were down,
And when they were only halfway up,
    They were neither up nor down.

PUSSY CAT, PUSSY CAT

Pussy cat, pussy cat, where have you been?

I've been to London to look at the queen.

Pussy cat, pussy cat, what did you there?

I frightened a little mouse under her chair.

THE QUEEN OF HEARTS

The Queen of Hearts
She made some tarts,
All on a summer's day;
The Knave of Hearts
He stole the tarts,
And took them clean away.

The King of Hearts
Called for the tarts,
And beat the Knave full sore;
The Knave of Hearts
Brought back the tarts,
And vowed he'd steal no more.

Monday's Child

Monday's child is fair of face,

Tuesday's child is full of grace,

Wednesday's child is full of woe,

Thursday's child has far to go,

Friday's child is loving and giving,

Saturday's child works hard for his living,

And the child that is born on the Sabbath day

Is bonny and blithe, and good and gay.

"What day was I born on, Mummy?" asked Small.

"You hatched out on a Thursday," said Mother Goose.

"Thursday's child has far to go," said Small. "Where have I got to go?"

"Somewhere hot and sunny for the winter, I should think," said Mother Goose. "Geese fly hundreds of miles in the winter."

"What day was I born on, Mummy?" asked Lucy.

"Thursday, the same as Small," said Mother Goose. "You all hatched out on Thursdays, one week after another."

"So we've all got far to go, then?" said Small.

"Yes," said Mother Goose.

"Can we all go together?" asked Small.

"Of course!" said Mother Goose. "Geese always fly together."

"That's all right, then," said Small.

LITTLE TOMMY TUCKER

Little Tommy Tucker,
  Sings for his supper:
What shall we give him?
  White bread and butter.
How shall he cut it
  Without a knife?
How will he be married
  Without a wife?

SIMPLE SIMON

Simple Simon met a pieman,
    Going to the fair;
Says Simple Simon to the pieman,
    Let me taste your ware.

Says the pieman to Simple Simon,
    Show me first your penny;
Says Simple Simon to the pieman,
    Indeed I have not any.

Mary, Mary, Quite Contrary

Mary, Mary, quite contrary,
How does your garden grow?
With silver bells and cockle shells,
And pretty maids all in a row.

ROUND AND ROUND THE GARDEN

Round and round the garden
Like a teddy bear;

Run your finger round your gosling's palm.

One step, two step,

"Jump" your fingers up his arm.

Tickly under there!

Tickle him under his arm.

Two sparrows were hopping around in the brambles. Boo wanted to say hello, so he ran up to one of them, flapping his wings. "Hello, birdie!" he shouted, but the sparrow flew away. So he ran up to the other sparrow. "Hello, other birdie!" he shouted, but that sparrow flew away, too.

"I don't think they heard me, Mummy," he said, sadly.

"You frightened them off," said Mother Goose. "You have to be quiet and gentle with birdies, and even then they sometimes fly away. They're very timid."

"What's timid?" asked Boo.

"It means they get frightened easily," said Mother Goose.

"I'm not timid, am I?" said Boo.

"Not very, dear, no," said Mother Goose.

Boo looked sad. "I was just being friendly," he said.

"I know you were," said Mother Goose. "But birdies still get scared, just like in this rhyme . . ."

ONCE I SAW A LITTLE BIRD

Once I saw a little bird
    Come hop, hop, hop,
And I cried, "Little bird,
    Will you stop, stop, stop?"

I was going to the window
    To say, "How do you do?"
But he shook his little tail
    And away he flew.

Oh Where, Oh Where?

Oh where, oh where has my little dog gone?
Oh where, oh where can he be?
With his ears cut short and his tail cut long,
Oh where, oh where is he?

OLD MOTHER HUBBARD

Old Mother Hubbard
Went to the cupboard,
To fetch her poor dog a bone;
But when she came there
The cupboard was bare
And so the poor dog had none.

FIDDLE-DE-DEE

Fiddle-de-dee, fiddle-de-dee,

The fly shall marry the humble-bee.

They went to the church, and married was she:

The fly has married the humble-bee.

"Did the fly and the humble-bee live happily ever after?" asked Lucy.

"I should think so," said Mother Goose.

"Could a spider marry a fly?" asked Small.

"Spiders eat flies," said Lucy. "She might eat him before the wedding."

"Could a dragonfly marry a worm?" asked Small.

"Worms are too slow," said Lucy. "The dragonfly would get bored waiting."

"A wasp could marry another wasp," said Small.

"And Lucy could marry a slug!" said Boo.

"Mummy!" cried Lucy. "Do I have to marry a slug?"

"Of course not, darling," said Mother Goose.

"Anyway," sniffed Lucy. "I'm going to marry Mummy."

"So am I," said Small.

"Me, too," said Boo.

"Right," said Mother Goose. "That's settled. Now, how about another rhyme?"

HICKORY, DICKORY, DOCK

Hickory, dickory, dock,

The mouse ran up the clock.

The clock struck one,

The mouse ran down,

Hickory, dickory, dock.

Cobbler, Cobbler

Cobbler, cobbler, mend my shoe.

Get it done by half-past two;

Stitch it up and stitch it down,

And then I'll give you half a crown.

Horsey, Horsey

Horsey, horsey, don't you stop,

Just let your feet go clippety-clop;

Your tail goes swish, and the wheels go round –

Giddy-up, you're homeward bound!

It was lunchtime, but Lucy was galloping up and down.

"Look, Mummy!" she called. "I'm being a horsey!"

"Giddy-up, dear," said Mother Goose. "Then come and eat grass with the rest of us."

"My feet are going clippety-clop!" shouted Lucy.

"Sounds more like flappety-flap to me," said Boo.

"I'm going to go really fast!" said Lucy.

"Watch where you're going," said Mother Goose, but Lucy ran straight into the river.

"Lucy's gone clippety-splosh!" said Small.

"Look, Mummy!" giggled Lucy. "I'm being a sea-horsey!"

"All right," laughed Mother Goose. "How about this for a new rhyme:

"Goosey-Lucy, don't you stop,

Just let your feet go clippety-splosh,

Your tail goes waggle and your wings go flap,

Now eat your lunch and have a nap!"

THIS IS THE WAY THE LADIES RIDE

*Cross your legs and sit your gosling over your top ankle, facing you.
Hold hands tightly, and jump her up and down to the rhyme. On the
last line, let her slip down gently over your toes to the ground.*

This is the way the ladies ride,

Trippety-trip, trippety-trip;

This is the way the gentlemen ride,

A-gallop-a-trot, a-gallop-a-trot;

This is the way the farmers ride,

Jiggety-jog, jiggety-jog;

And when they come to a hedge – they jump over!

And when they come to a slippery place – they

    scramble, scramble,

        Tumble-down Dick!

To Market, To Market

To market, to market, to buy a fat pig,

Home again, home again, jiggety-jig;

To market, to market, to buy a fat hog,

Home again, home again, jiggety-jog.

To market, to market,

To buy a plum bun:

Home again, home again,

Market is done.

Jack Be Nimble

Jack be nimble,
Jack be quick,
Jack jump over
The candlestick.

"I could jump over a candlestick," said Boo.

"So could I," said Small.

"You couldn't," said Boo. "You can't jump over anything."

"Yes, I can!" said Small, and he started to cry.

"Jump over that puddle, then," said Boo.

Small waddled slowly up to the puddle and stopped.

"See," said Boo. "You can't."

"I don't want to jump," said Small. "I want to look at the clouds."

"The clouds are in the sky, silly," said Boo.

"No, they're not," said Small. "They're in the puddle."

Boo looked at the puddle. "Oh!" he said. "Are there always clouds in the puddles?"

"Yes," said Small. "But they go away if you splash them."

"I won't splash, then," said Boo.

And they stared at the clouds in the puddle until Mother Goose called them over for tea.

LITTLE JUMPING JOAN

Here am I,
Little Jumping Joan;
When nobody's with me
I'm all alone.

FROGGY, FROGGY

Froggy, froggy.
Hoppity-hop!
When you get to the sea
You do not stop.
Plop!

Goosey, Goosey Gander

Goosey, goosey gander,
    Whither shall I wander?
Upstairs and downstairs
    And in my lady's chamber.
There I met an old man
    Who would not say his prayers.
I took him by the left leg
    And threw him down the stairs.

TWINKLE, TWINKLE, LITTLE STAR

Twinkle, twinkle, little star,
How I wonder what you are!
Up above the world so high,
Like a diamond in the sky.

Small was having a sneezy day.

"A-a-a-*choo!*" he went. "A-a-a-*choo!* Mummy! I can't stop sneezing. A-a-a-*choo!*"

Mother Goose felt his forehead. "You don't feel hot," she said, "so I don't think you've got a cold. There must be some dust in the air that's making you sneeze."

"Why is there dust in the air?" asked Lucy.

"The old lady must be doing her spring cleaning," said Mother Goose.

"What old lady?" asked Boo.

"The one who cleans the sky. Haven't I told you about her?"

"No," said the goslings.

"Settle down, then," said Mother Goose, "and listen . . ."

THERE WAS AN OLD WOMAN
TOSSED UP IN A BASKET

There was an old woman tossed up in a basket,

Seventeen times as high as the moon;

Where she was going I couldn't but ask it,

For in her hand she carried a broom.

Old woman, old woman, old woman, quoth I,

Where are you going to up so high?

To brush the cobwebs off the sky!

May I go with you?

Aye, by-and-by.

Wee Willie Winkie

Wee Willie Winkie runs through the town,

Upstairs and downstairs in his night-gown,

Rapping at the window, crying through the lock,

Are the children all in bed, for now it's eight o'clock?

DIDDLE, DIDDLE, DUMPLING

Diddle, diddle, dumpling, my son John,

Went to bed with his trousers on;

One shoe off, and one shoe on,

Diddle, diddle, dumpling, my son John.

STAR WISH

Star light, star bright,
First star I see tonight,
I wish I may, I wish I might,
Have the wish I wish tonight.

It was bedtime. The goslings were looking up at the stars.

"What do you wish, Lucy?" asked Boo.

"I wish I was a ballerina," said Lucy.

"Geese can't be ballerinas," said Boo, "can they, Mummy?"

"They can if they wish hard enough," said Mother Goose.

"What do you wish, Small?" asked Lucy.

"I wish I could fly," said Small.

"But you can fly, silly," said Lucy. "You're a goose!"

"Oh, yes," said Small. "I forgot."

"What do you wish, Mummy?" asked Boo.

"I wish we could all get some sleep," said Mother Goose.

So they did.

❧ INDEX OF FIRST LINES ❧

Claude was a dog. Claude was a small dog.
Claude was a small, plump dog.

Claude was a small, plump dog who liked
wearing a beret and a lovely red jumper.

Claude lived with his owners Mr and Mrs Shinyshoes
and his best friend Sir Bobblysock.

Every day, when Mr and Mrs Shinyshoes went out to work,
Claude and Sir Bobblysock would get ready to have an
adventure.

Where will they go today?

To GEORGIA,
THOMAS, EUAN
and CONNOR

Thank you
to my friend
CHARLOTTE REED,
the original
Giddy Kipper

HODDER CHILDREN'S BOOKS

First published in Great Britain in 2016
by Hodder and Stoughton

Text and illustrations © Alex T. Smith 2016

The moral rights of the
author/illustrator have been asserted.

All rights reserved.

A CIP catalogue record of this book
is available from the British Library.

ISBN: 9781 444 90367 6

10 9 8 7 6 5 4 3 2 1

Printed and bound in China.

Hodder Children's Books
An imprint of
Hachette Children's Group
Part of Hodder and Stoughton
Carmelite House
50 Victoria Embankment
London EC4Y 0DZ

An Hachette UK Company
www.hachette.co.uk

www.hachettechildrens.co.uk

CLAUDE

All at Sea

Alex T. Smith

One day, Claude had been painting
and now he needed a bath.

Sir Bobblysock said so, and he knew **ALL** about these things.

So Claude stashed his paintbrushes in his beret and turned on the taps in the bathroom. Then he went to find his bath toys.

Downstairs, Sir Bobblysock busied himself with his knick-knacks.

Nobody
remembered the water until...

DRIP!

DRIP!

DRIP!

BATHROOM

...it was too late.

WHOOOSH!

went the water.

'Yikes!' went Claude, and he grabbed Sir Bobblysock and **leapt** into the bathtub as a huge

wave carried them

down
the
stairs...

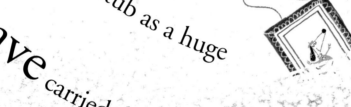

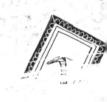

along the street...

and into the
deep blue sea.

SPLASH!

Claude had **never** sailed a bathtub on the ocean before.

It was **very** wet and **stonking** good fun!

Whilst Claude looked at all the splashy water,
Sir Bobbysock busied himself reading some signs.

They seemed to be **jolly important**
and all about someone called Nigel.

'I wonder who Nigel is?' said Claude.

But before Sir Bobblysock could tell him...

...a GIGANTIC
sea monster
(called Nigel)

suddenly appeared and...

GOBBLED
them up!

It was very dark and very damp in Nigel's tummy.

Claude was getting a bit scared and

Sir Bobblysock's stitches started to quiver

when voices came from the darkness...

Claude LOVED helping, so he hopped on board
Captain Poopdeck's boat. He emptied his beret out
to see if he had anything useful in there.

He did.

First, they tried the stepladder.
But that didn't work. It was too short.

'We could climb out using the rope!'
said Cindy. It was a **very** good idea,
but that didn't work either because
it was in such a

t a n g l e.

The Giddy Kipper

'This is a **disaster**,'
cried Captain Poopdeck.

'We're **trapped**!'
gasped Cindy Seaweed.

'We are going to be stuck in here
for ever!' yelped Sir Bobblysock.

'**And ever**!' said Barry, helpfully.

Sir Bobblysock's knees knocked
and he started to hiccup.
Suddenly Claude had a
wonderful idea...

'If we give Nigel the hiccups, we might fly out and not be stuck in here any more?'

Everyone thought this was a super idea, so they all grabbed a brush and started tickling...

Out on the ocean,
Nigel's tummy started
to **twitch**,
and **wiggle**,
and **jiggle** until...

HICCUP!

Everyone flew out.

'Oh dear!' said Nigel,

'I didn't mean to gobble you all up.
I don't usually eat
seagulls or people
or dogs or socks.
I much prefer
Seaweed Sandwiches.
The problem is, I just can't
see very well.'

Claude wagged his tail. He could do some more helping!

He quickly reached into his beret and handed
Nigel the enormous glasses he'd found
in there earlier.

'Thank you!' said Nigel. 'Now I'll never gobble up anyone ever again!'

'HOORAY FOR CLAUDE!' everyone shouted.

By now, it was getting late, and Claude and Sir Bobblysock had to get home, so they said goodbye to their new friends and promised to come back and play next bathtime.

When Mr and Mrs Shinyshoes came home, they couldn't understand why their bath was in the kitchen.

'Do you think Claude knows anything about this?' said Mrs Shinyshoes.

'Let's ask him when he wakes up!'
said Mr Shinyshoes.

Claude smiled a little smile. Of course he knew why their bath was in the kitchen. And we do too, don't we?

THE END.